BUSINESS OF *Mom*

Lori Guerrero

Business of Mom
By Lori Guerrero
Published by Beverly Hills Publishing
468 Camden Drive
Beverly Hills, CA 90210
www.beverlyhillspublishing.com

Copyright © 2020 Beverly Hills Publishing Firm, Beverly Hills, California. All rights reserved.

ISBN: 978-1-7360900-1-5

In no way is it legal to reproduce, duplicate, or transmit any part of this document in either electronic means or in printed format. Recording of this publication is strictly prohibited and any storage of this document is not allowed unless with written permission from the publisher. All rights reserved.

The information provided herein is stated to be truthful and consistent, in that any liability, in terms of inattention or otherwise, by any usage or abuse of any policies, processes, or directions contained within is the solitary and utter responsibility of the recipient reader. Under no circumstances will any legal responsibility or blame be held against the publisher for any reparation, damages, or monetary loss due to the information herein, either directly or indirectly. Respective authors own all copyrights not held by the publisher. The information herein is offered for informational purposes solely and is universal, as so. The presentation of the information is without contract or any type of guarantee assurance.

The trademarks that are used are without any consent, and the publication of the trademark is without permission or backing by the trademark owner. All trademarks and brands within this book are for clarifying purposes only and are the owned by the owners themselves, not affiliated with this document

---

The information and descriptions presented in this book and in the Business of Mom newsletters and website are intended for adults, age 18 and over, and are solely for informational and educational purposes. Lori Guerrero does not give legal, psychological, or financial advice. Before beginning any new business or personal development routine, or if you have specific legal, psychological, or medical concerns, a medical, financial, legal, or other professional should be consulted.

Any reproduction, republication, or other distribution of this work, including, without limitation, the duplication, copying, scanning, uploading, and making available via the internet or any other means, without the express permission of the publisher is illegal and punishable by law, and the knowing acquisition of an unauthorized reproduction of this work may subject the acquirer to liability. Please purchase only authorized electronic or print editions of this work and do not participate in or encourage electronic piracy of copyrighted materials. Your support of the author's rights is appreciated.

This document is geared towards providing exact and reliable information with regards to the topic and issue covered. The publication is sold with the idea that the publisher is not required to render accounting, officially permitted, or otherwise, qualified services. If advice is necessary, legal or professional, a practiced individual in the profession should be ordered.

– *From a Declaration of Principles which was accepted and approved equally by a Committee of the American Bar Association and a Committee of Publishers and Associations.*

Business of Mom is dedicated to my family.

To my husband, Alex, for loving me and supporting me through every new crazy idea I have.

To my children and grandchildren: Madison with her precious Kennedy and Bradley, Brayden, Alexis, Aaron and Abby. YOU are my world, my legacy and the reason that I exist in this world. I am blessed to be called your MOM.

To God, and my guardian angel in heaven, my Dad. I know that without your blessings and your careful watch over me, nothing would be possible.

Table of Contents

Introduction 7

Chapter 1
Service at the Heart 11

Chapter 2
It's Not About Money 17

Chapter 3
Permission to Dream 27

Chapter 4
What Would You Do If You Knew You Could Not Fail? 33

Chapter 5
Exploration 43

Chapter 6
The Benefits of Failure 49

Chapter 7
Open The Dialogue 57

Chapter 8
Planning Mastery 69

Chapter 9
Overcoming Obstacles 77

Chapter 10
Something Can Derail You 85

Chapter 11
Roll With It 95

Chapter 12
Celebrate The Wins! 105

Chapter 13
Your Legacy & Mastering 'Doing It All' 113

Introduction

> "What exactly can you do for me that
> I can't do for myself?"
> *Rosie The Riveter Pamphlet*

Throughout history, women have been resilient doers. They've consistently played fundamental leadership roles, often assuming a responsibility to "do it all."

During war times, not only were women left without their fathers, husbands, sons, and brothers, women remained at home with all of the work. They took care of the children and the home, became proficient cooks and cleaners, managed the finances, and learned to repair their vehicles. All the while, many held jobs outside the home to make ends meet.

Despite this history of hard work, ability to juggle numerous challenges, and accomplishment on multiple levels inside and outside the home, today's woman can still, somehow, find herself struggling with a limiting belief that she can only have a great family if she doesn't invest in her career. Something tells me you know what I'm talking about! How is it that the nagging doubt can so quickly pop into our brains?

As women, we seem to be born with an innate sense that we cannot have it all. Through this message, I hope to help you understand how wrong this is. As important, I intend to help you really see how you can set an example for other women that having it all is, in fact, quite possible.

Life is too short to wait on your dreams. Your dreams are 100 percent attainable. You can set up your own Business of Mom.

How do you think the world would be different if women were able to stop holding themselves back? I think that that world would be such a beautiful, more dynamic place. Do you agree? Imagine if the most talented, multitasking, constantly juggling mind of a mother were to be inside the leader of the world? If the mind of a mother were running our businesses, foreign relations, and making the laws, I think the world that we live in would be very different.

The mind of a mother is able to understand the needs of children and the family and how they integrate into the workplace, and business. For instance, the mind of a mother knows that the worst time to schedule a conference call is between the hours of 5 p.m. and 7 p.m. when she is trying to get dinner on the table. The mind of a mother has the unique ability to see the bigger picture and consider multiple perspectives.

If everyone worked and ran companies and the world with the mind of a mom, the world would have a global, family-oriented society.

As for me, I grew up watching "Mr. Mom" with Michael Keaton. In the show, the father loses his job and the mother has to go to work.

Seeing this was a surprise to me, because I grew up in an era when mothers stayed home with the children while the father held a job outside the home. I viewed this family structure as "just the way it is."

Introduction

In my generation, it was always seen as ideal if the family was financially stable enough for the mother to stay home with the children.

However, so much has changed since then. Today, in most two-parent families both spouses work outside the home. Challenges abound for those who are single parents, as I was at one point. (Yes, all of this information is just as relevant for my single-parent readers! More on this is ahead.)

Financially, I have the ability to stay home with my children without the need to work outside the home. However, I have done enough soul-searching to learn that being a mother is only a part of the role that I was meant to play in life. You, too, may feel you are destined for more.

I'm not going to say that I am an expert at "having it all," but I think that I have reached a place in my life at which I have figured out how to be fulfilled beyond my reproductive purposes. I can truly say that I have found that balance and fulfillment.

My hope is that the encouragement in this book can help you gain that same sense of fulfillment, which you can then model to others.

Note: At the end of each chapter, I've provided you a page of action steps, called "Thoughts To Think About."

I recommend you read each chapter and complete the steps that make the content more personal to YOU. (I know, I know. You're so busy. But trust me – this will be time well spent!)

Completing each chapter's action steps can help you become more equipped, focused, and dedicated to seeing your vision through to completion.

I'm so excited for you, mom. Let's get going!

CHAPTER 1:

Service at the Heart

> "Everybody can be great . . . because anybody can serve. You don't have to have a college degree to serve. You don't have to make your subject and verb agree to serve. You only need a heart full of grace. A soul generated by love."
>
> Martin Luther King Jr.

In my younger years, like many women I struggled with the fear of being a "bad mom" for wanting to achieve something outside of my family. I now know what gives me purpose and meaning, which humans all crave.

I grew up in a small town and went into college unsure of what exactly I wanted to be. My two tracks were either nursing or teaching, mainly because my whole family is made up of nurses and teachers.

Growing up, my father was a cowboy and our family always lived paycheck to paycheck. We never dreamed of having anything outside of that. In our view, that was just the way the world worked for us.

I was told that I was meant to go to college and learn a trade or get a degree so that I could live a normal life, per se. When I finally got into college, I found out very quickly that I loved to serve others. Whichever career path I were to take, I knew that I would do well in either teaching or nursing. It wasn't long before I realized my deep love for those professions.

As it turned out, I went into nursing and realized I had skills in management. I was only in nursing for a couple of years before I became a manager, then a director, and finally landed in hospital administration rather quickly after graduating.

Nevertheless, I began to feel like my job was burning me out. I decided that I wanted to branch out and do something a little different. I decided on teaching. For quite some time, I taught healthcare sciences Monday through Friday while continuing to practice nursing on the weekends.

In my mind, through teaching and nursing, I was getting the best of both worlds. In both of these professions, I soon realized that so many improvements were possible in our society. Among them were how healthcare was delivered and how students were educated with regard to health care.

I found myself envisioning a world that featured a better way to care for and educate patients and students.

About five years ago, I couldn't stop my visions of what was possible in healthcare and education. I began to have conversations with my business partner. We discussed how we could improve healthcare delivery in ways that people need it, and enable them to handle their self-care more effectively.

I told him, "Let's just do this ourselves."

My vision was very small. I wanted to impact a corner of a nearby low-income community with a single medical facility, one emergency room, and one small hospital. The people in that area were so marginalized. I wanted to fix that – to enable the residents to truly depend on us to be available for them with the best care possible.

Three years later, we had created eight facilities, two hospitals, and jobs for more than 300 employees.

One idea exploded out of the vision of wanting to best serve our patients. This empire sprouted solely on the basis of wanting to do good on behalf of others, with our employees and patients. I have faith that this effort will only continue to grow.

I'll bet if you consider your area of the world, your own expertise, and your sphere of influence, you could envision, influence, or invent what doesn't yet exist – enhancements that could improve lives and bring you fulfillment you would otherwise never realize!

Throughout this effort, I have continued to study. I have attained a double master's in business administration and healthcare administration as well as a bachelor's degree in nursing. I'm always continuing to learn and study, as there is never a limit to all you can learn.

Recently, I've enrolled in classes to accelerate my knowledge on the legal side of the healthcare world, education spurred by the need to handle some legal certifications related to healthcare.

I feel as though it is my mission to continually learn to better myself to use my new skills either towards the business side of things, family side of things, patient focused things and so on.

At the end of the day, when people ask me, "Hey, what do you do?" I simply say, "I'm a nurse." My daughter corrects me with admonitions such as, "Now, Mom, you're not just a nurse. You own all these ERs. You own these hospitals. You run this company."

She may be right, but in my view, nursing is at the core. All the rest grows from there. If there is one thing that I do for certain, it's serving others.

People often ask me, "Well, what do you do for *yourself?*" I always end up saying, "Well, this *is* what I do for myself."

Serving others *is* me and it is what is fulfilling to me. I have a passion to serve when I wake up in the morning – whether it's serving my family, serving the employees who take care of our patients, or asking a sick patient in the lobby, "How can I help you today?"

The world is bursting with situations and environments where we can feel like a number, just another person amid in sea of billions of people. It is easy to feel lost and unimportant. Particularly when we are ill and suffering, or perhaps struggling with grief or loss, it is easy to see how feelings can become overwhelming and people can lose hope.

Saying to those in need, "How can I help you?" is the mission that I have committed myself to every day.

If each of us simply takes a moment to really see people – and connect to them to the point even briefly to let them know somebody cares – this can make a massive difference to them!

TO THINK ABOUT

1. When you were younger, what did you want to be? Why? If you could be anything now, what would it be?

2. Who (or what demographic) would you most like to serve? Why?

3. Aside from occupations, from the 30,000-foot level, what overall contribution would you dearly love to make to the world?

4. How do you want people to remember you?

5. Can you make a connection between your answers that can give you direction?

CHAPTER 2:
It's Not About Money

> "Don't make money your goal. Instead, pursue the things you love doing, and then do them so well that people can't take their eyes off you."
> *Maya Angelou*

When we started the business, people didn't see me as a leader within the financial realm of healthcare. In discussions, when I'd ask a question, at times men and women shared comments such as, "Oh, you're so cute when it comes to the finances, Lori."

To be honest, I can read financial statements and interpret financial forecasting with the best of them. It's just that money has never been the driving force for me. My focus is on simply doing the right things and believing that everything else will work itself out.

I'm not just a cute little woman taking a job. For me, it is always about building the project, fulfilling needs, and doing something to help make life better for somebody.

Women are conditioned to endure this type of kindhearted but misplaced comment that implies we don't know what we are doing. But we need to rise above it and not dwell on it, because the opposite is usually true.

I believe women have the ability to see the bigger picture. Sometimes the right things to do have financial consequences, but that's not what is important. Yes, financial freedom is rewarding, but that's not the driving force behind all of what we were doing.

In my view, I believe that this mentality shift of looking at what the money is used *for*, not the money itself, is what helped us become successful. Money is not our focus, people are.

In the healthcare world, specifically the ER world, the day-to-day tasks are extremely serious. By nature, employees can frequently come across as though they are in bad moods. It is simply a fact of the work. Those operating outside of this line of work might assume the opposite, that nurses and doctors are always happy to be there, and happy to help their patients.

The reality is that the medical staff is working long shifts. They've taken care of countless patients over a seemingly endless 12-hour shift. When patients and loved ones interact with them, the doctors and nurses may not have eaten in hours, and they haven't taken breaks. They likely haven't even had a recent opportunity to use the restroom. They can come across as grumpy. Those who interact with them could be tempted to take this attitude personally. This would be a mistake. It's important to understand that the work they do is downright hard on them, and this can affect their attitude.

In contrast, much of the time I enjoyed these challenging experiences. I was happy to help my patients. In the midst of a big ER, I would look outside the box to solve my patients' problems.

If I encountered a patient with a major need, I often sought out like-minded professionals who also put the patient above everything else. I quickly found out that you must find collaborators in the workplace who support your dreams, goals, and mindset. A work family must be one that is supportive, with each member complementing the desires and dreams of the others on the team.

As I surrounded myself with these people, our like-mindedness spurred forward-thinking conversations about how we could leverage our desire to take the best care of patients in the ER.

In addition to our work together at the hospital, several of us worked for other companies, and having those extra roles fueled a collective vision for exciting, new opportunities. The more we conversed, the more we realized that we held knowledge that could help us carry out business better than the status quo. We knew we could take care of these patients better than the way other companies were doing it.

As a team, we determined to give it our best shot. A business partnership began. Of course, patients were the focus.

This desire to care for and provide the best service to patients was simply a workplace extension of the care I gave my family.

Since taking that leap, though our focus has remained on our patients, we have profited. Today, each of our seven freestanding emergency room facilities in the Dallas-Fort Worth area gross at least $20 million a year. Net profit is three to five million dollars, per facility.

This solid financial stability enables us to attract partnerships with funding companies. We educate them, gain their trust and secure their investment over the long haul. This fuels more business growth, and increases our ability to help patients.

It is without a doubt that healthcare is a big business, so it is not surprising that so many make it out to be about the dollars. In our effort, we've really tried to stay focused on building relationships with our patients and serving them.

With the current U.S. model, it is incredibly expensive to take care of people. American healthcare, specifically, is uniquely expensive and finance-focused. Patients can become chained to their insurance companies.

We try, day in and day out, to make sure that we're focusing on the money being sacrificed by the patients rather than the money being spent by the insurance companies. Our goal is to make our care worth it for our patients. We aim to give them the best value for their dollar.

The point of expressing all of this is to highlight the fact that none of this would have been possible if I told myself "Oh, I can't have it all" or, "I have to sacrifice some part of myself to do this." That mindset only limits what is possible for you.

When my husband asks me things such as, "How much can you realistically take on?" I answer that I will just keep building and creating the structures around the systems until I can't manage it anymore. For me, I never wonder when this is all going to end for me. It could go back to nothing tomorrow or it could grow to be 10 times bigger by tomorrow. I'm open either way.

In this, the key to success is finding that balance in your life. It is finding the sweet spot where your family is nurtured, and where you are nurtured by your family, which makes you able to have this kind of drive and passion in your career.

By the way, don't even think that single mothers can't pull this off, too. That fact is, I wasn't always married. When I met Alex, my husband, he told me that one of the things he admired about me was the fact that I was a single mother working two jobs and raising two kids all on my own without the support system that a family unit brings.

If you are a single mother, take solace in your strength. Your strength will be admired by the right people and you will get past all the debris.

Having balance does not require having your family fit with tradition. You can experience a "have-it-all" life, balance and happy as a single mother with a great career and happy kids. It is all about how you adopt the proper mentality and create that structure around you.

My family is just as amazing and challenging as my work is. In earlier years, I envisioned having two, maybe three kids at the most. Now I have five!

Now that my youngest is four, I have this feeling that perhaps someday a child out there will need a home – and that home will be with us.

My first marriage was not a failure by any means, we were just two very different people. I like to refer to it as a really great learning experience for me. I learned things I should and shouldn't do. I learned what I did want and what I didn't. I learned who I really was at my core. All of that led me to finding out what I really wanted out of life *before* trying to build a healthy relationship.

My ex-husband and I have a wonderful relationship now. I value the fact that we are both self-driven people who serve as healthy models for our children.

My two oldest children, from my first marriage, are 27 and 17 as I write this book, and both of them are doing extremely well.

My oldest, a daughter, is also a nurse and is in graduate school. She has two children, so I have two grandchildren who are six and four years old, my precious Kennedy and Bradley. My daughter is actually a role model for me. I am so proud of what a great mother and wife she has grown up to be.

My 17-year-old son is here at home with me. As he prepares to graduate from high school, my heart is full to see the warm and giving spirit he has and know that he is going to do great things.

My 11-year-old is very much like me in the fact that she is a very driven young lady. She worries more than most 40-year-olds who have double mortgages and credit card debt. She keeps us in order.

So much is yet to be determined about my 4 and 6 year olds. Their personalities are developing daily, and I am excited to see what their full potential will be.

I think animals are incredibly important to the family. We have three babies that I love on every day. For me, my animals are my relaxation and therapy. They, too, require quite a bit of my attention.

At times, I take my Boston Terrier and French Bulldog to work with me. In my view, it is very important to nurture a pet-friendly environment in the hospital atmosphere. We've adopted this policy because we see so many patients who have only their pets as their family. If the patient is sick, it is important for them to have support alongside them.

It is as important to create a system that works for doctors and nurses, as it is for our patients. A system may be a schedule. It may be a process. It may be people.

On that note, what makes the systems work are the people who are committed to making them work. Without the people nothing would work. This can be seen in any organization, at home and at work.

Perhaps my kids must be patient with me if I'm rushing to drop them off at practice. Maybe the babysitter or my husband picks up the kids or drops them off. Maybe the work family, or the pets, have to wait. Fine tuning the systems is a process. Patience is required.

In your career, it doesn't have to be, "Oh, I've got to keep it all going. I've got to just keep adding more and more and more to my plate." You need to establish the right system that supports you and keeps it all intact.

In life, we must become masters of delegation. We can do a lot for people, but as individuals, we can't do it all. It's about that give and take. You may ask someone to help you with something today. Tomorrow, you may need to help them with something. We each scratch the other's back, helping them accomplish what they cannot do on their own.

We're all in this world together, and we must embrace it. We are not alone, so we need to stop trying to do it all by ourselves!

If you know you have bottled up potential and ideas that you keep pushing further down, take this as a sign that you can turn this around.

Once you get to the end of the book, you can put it down and start your own company. You can do something for you and you only without feeling guilty. All that you need is inside of you already.

TO THINK ABOUT

1. How comfortable do you feel about leaning on others to help with family chores and child-related tasks?

2. If you feel discomfort, what is the actual cause? How can you address this cause?

3. What small steps can you take this week to bring you to a place where you can begin to release and trust, solving one problem for you and for others?

4. What hitches might be unique, or more pronounced, to those with a different marital status than yours? Identify one mother from this group whom you can assist this week.

5. What characteristics do you want to exhibit to your family and others through your cultivation of your dream? How can addressing your challenges present these characteristics?

CHAPTER 3:
Permission to Dream

> "People are working harder than ever, but because they lack clarity and vision, they aren't getting very far."
> *Dr. Stephen R. Covey*

You have permission to envision a future that can be different than you've ever imagined. It's definitely OK to want to do more than you are currently doing in your day-to-day life. Some women go their whole lives without reaching this first step toward personal fulfillment. Don't be one of them!

It starts when you give yourself permission to want something more.

You are unique. Nobody has the same "gift mix" that you have. To sit on your potential is keeping a lid on what makes you special and what only you can contribute to the world with your amazing flair. Your dream helps you realize your potential.

It's so important to reiterate that when giving yourself permission to dream, you're not sacrificing your family. In fact, research shows that this path might even make you a better mom.

According to a Harvard Business School study, Kathleen McGinn and colleagues found that upon reaching adulthood, daughters of working mothers were 1.29 times more likely to achieve a supervisory role and more likely to have higher salaries. [1]

According to McGinn, "People still have this belief that when moms are employed, it's somehow detrimental to their children, (but) our finding that maternal employment doesn't affect kids' happiness in adulthood is really important."

By simply having conversations with your kids about your dreams, you inspire them to think about their own dreams. You can ask them what they want to be or how they want to impact the world. You are helping to shape their goals and their future by talking about and thinking about what they want to do.

Even if you've abandoned your dream or you haven't given yourself permission to dream before, think back to a time when you were a child, before the world got to you, before all of life got locked in as "this is what I'm supposed to be."

Some of us as children dreamed of being a mom – that supermom, that overachiever mom, that soccer mom, volleyball mom – but most of us dreamed of doing something outside of that, too.

We've all been asked the question, "What do you want to be when you grow up?" Even if you thought, "Oh, I want to be a supermom," and you got that, that's a huge accomplishment. Congratulations!

But remember that child-rearing is a temporary task. It may be hard to imagine, but your little ones one day will be established adults who will live on their own.

Recall in high school, you probably had a career in mind based on your interests, your skills, what were you good at. I doubt that you wrote on career aptitude tests and college entrance surveys that you wanted to be a mom.

So, what did you pick back then?

Let's unpack it further, so you have ample food for thought: What did you dream about as a child? What did you like to play? Did you play school? Did you play gift shop? Did you play attorney? What was your favorite thing to do as a child?

You have so many additional gifts. Begin investing in them now. Ensure that you have opportunities now and in the future to serve using your talents.

Perhaps you are gifted with empathy and are rejuvenated when you are able to help a friend find her way out of a confusing or painful situation.

Maybe you love animals and always dreamed of a workplace surrounded by them.

Maybe you like the consistency of working with numbers. Could you see yourself helping people manage their money?

One woman, at a young age, saw herself simply as a business woman who would carry a briefcase and run a company. This set an under-the-radar goal that helped her push past naysayers who doubted her, and served as a model of achievement to her husband and her now-grown children – whom she successfully raised while working. They are her biggest cheerleaders.

By now, you get the drill. You simply need to establish your own starting point with your own vision.

Establishing a potential job is a good first step. It can lead you toward finding a life path that can take you beyond the status quo, to a level of deep personal satisfaction and service to others.

So get going. You can begin by talking about your deepest dreams, feelings, and ideas with your spouse, a close friend, or your children. Speaking about them can give value and life to the potential deep inside you.

This is an important step, because feelings not expressed can build up. Resentment can be stuck beneath them. Expressing your dreams can promote a healthy relationship with your family, with your spouse, and with your children. It can open a support system for you that may help you with your next steps.

I encourage you to keep your family updated on your victories and struggles regarding your vision or enterprise. Listen to their ideas. This ensures they have some "skin in the game" and that they are not lost in the shuffle. Listen to their less-than-positive input, too, because whether you change your path or not, just knowing you hear them can reduce or remove any potential resentment.

If you haven't given yourself permission to dream, here's your permission slip! It's time to get busy, and certainly not feel guilty. The world needs all aspects of your God-given talents.

Thoughts
TO THINK ABOUT

1. Why do people sometimes feel guilty about having a job and also being a mother?

2. Why do you think some people fear sharing a dream?

3. Who might be the first person with whom you'd choose to share details of your dream?

4. How can your family enhance your ability to embark on a new path en route to your dream?

5. What reasons can you think of to explain why adult children of working mothers see such success?

CHAPTER 4:
What Would You Do If You Knew You Could Not Fail?

> "You can dance in the storm. Don't wait for the rain to be over before because it might take too long. You can do it now. Wherever you are, right now, you can start, right now; this very moment."
> Israelmore Ayivor

Earlier in this book, we talked about the fact that many of us had a dream growing up. However, the mistake we can make is that we let it remain as merely a dream.

To get to where we want to go, we must take at least a couple steps to dip our toes into the water of our imagination.

If we don't explore a little bit, we may end up dreaming forever.

When you bring yourself into the reality of your dreams, you may realize that the water is too cold. Then you will realize whether or not that dream is a reality for you. Exploring is a way to test things out to see what you do and don't like.

You may have dreamed of being a preschool or kindergarten teacher, but when you got in the classroom, you may have been dismayed by the objectional duties – wiping boogers or helping to potty train. Those less-than-desirable duties were not what you thought would occupy your time.

In a situation like this, high-achieving women can get stuck continuing to push through, driven to not give up until they accomplish everything. But at times, reality can be telling you that your choice isn't the best fit.

Give yourself permission to adopt a trial mindset from the start. You are testing the waters, and just exploring. Knowing this in advance allows you to release any unattainable expectations that aren't based in reality. It sets you up to consider an occupation, not evaluate it against an unreachable benchmark available only in your dreams. You'll never be satisfied.

An exploration mindset gives you an opportunity to be able to say, OK, I've dreamed of it, but now let me test the waters a little bit. Let me see, before I jump right into the deep end. Let me start in the shallow end of the pool and make sure this is really what I want.

This may mean asking your family how they feel about your dream, as well as how it impacts everything else in your life.

The best way to do this is to map it all out on paper. Write down how you think your dream would look and then see if reality matches up to what you put down on paper.

To start, list who you have around you that, if you had to stay late at work, could pitch in and help you with the kids? Or if you had to leave early one morning, what would that look like, as far as lunches, for example? Determine if you can plan lunches and dinners out by delegating it with a schedule, map, or plan.

For instance, what would your week look like if you were to go back to work three days a week, or two days a week? How would it impact your family? Get it all on paper. The key is to put it all down on paper along with what the goal is.

In accessing these goals, you must have a "pull cord," the emergency button that lets you know when you need to stop and reevaluate.

When things are spinning out of control, what does that emergency button look like for you? It is important to write down these outcomes you fear, as well. With them, you can indicate what remedy to choose when things get sidetracked or start to go badly.

In your life, your roadblocks might be family, friends, or school. A solution might be to set up a backup plan. Perhaps you can establish a team of moms in your community. This could allow you to trade off with other moms in carpooling to soccer practice, for instance. You would serve your week, and then mom number two would serve her week, and mom number three could cover your week if you become too busy.

Creating something tangible such as a ride share gives you free time to focus on your aspirations. The best part of this is the fact that the other moms would embrace these systems, as they also have other things going on that they could use some extra time with, as well.

As you set up this mom team (that can definitely involve dads, too!), all those involved will be empowered by newfound freedom that all parties desperately need.

These types of contingency plans allow you to begin the process of making your dream a reality.

At this point, your dream is out there, but it's in the clouds, waiting for you to bring it down to Earth. Ask yourself: who are the people that my dream will impact? How can they contribute to helping me get there?

When you keep your dreams in the clouds floating in the abyss, they're not truly attainable. This is why it is so important to put all of your thoughts down on paper in front of you.

By writing down all you would like to achieve, you make your aspirations more real. You transition them from a daydream to reality.

Research has found that vivid, written descriptions of goals can boost success in reaching them, according to a *Forbes* article by Mark Murphy, CEO of Leadership IQ.[2]

"People who very vividly describe or picture their goals are anywhere from 1.2 to 1.4 times more likely to successfully accomplish their goals than people who don't," Murphy wrote. Part of this is due to the fact that the written word can be revisited, and repetition can help with recollection.

Let's say I wanted to be a children's author. After getting it all down in writing, I might realize that even though I may have a college education, I may want to take some creative writing classes, or enroll in another type of course online that might enhance my opportunity for success in this particular field first.

Including some baby steps in order to drill down to your goals, actually writing them down, sharing them with your family, and sharing them with your support system will create a concrete foundation to support your choice.

As Murphy asserted, writing things down makes your mind more efficient by helping you focus on the truly important stuff. Your goals absolutely should qualify as truly important stuff!

Every time that I started a new venture, I mapped it out and put it on paper. This makes something so complicated become simple. That's the point. It *must* be simple to be attainable – even if it isn't at face value. It must be in baby steps, or it's just going to seem too overwhelming to go from one extreme to the other.

Without making these first steps, many women fail to achieve their dreams through comparing their experience with someone else's. Many feel like they should be able to go straight from where they are to where they need to be because, on the outside, it may look easy for other people.

Many women get stuck on the thought of "Where do I even begin?" The answer is to start small by beginning the exploration of how to get to where you want to be.

It's really about doing your homework, doing your research, in order to then make these little steps and add these little building blocks along the way.

As life goes, I have had many ventures and ideas that I thought would be a big success that turned out not to pan out.

For instance, I was enamored with the idea to open a restaurant. I took the baby steps of partnering with someone who had owned a restaurant before, and who had the experience needed to jumpstart my dream.

I invested money and time into this dream, without a grip on what the restaurant lingo was, what equipment was needed, and pretty much everything that went into opening a restaurant.

About halfway through the project, I started looking at the statistics of failure, and I started having this dooming feeling of, "what have I gotten myself into?"

I continued more research into what makes a restaurant thrive and I learned that food hardly makes any money - the key was to get alcohol on the menu.

Sure enough, the restaurant business was not something that worked for me, and the restaurant ultimately didn't make it. However, it gave me a great experience in determining whether that dream actually was something realistic for me. Now that I've gone through it, the yearning for that experience is gone, my zest for being in the restaurant business is gone, and I learned that it actually wasn't my dream, as I had previously thought.

In this experience, instead of dipping my toes in the water, I jumped right into the deep end and faced the possibility of drowning. This experience taught me more than ever that I need to do my due diligence before entering into such a commitment.

If I would have really researched more into who else is running the business, looked at who I was going to be working with, working for, etc. and determining whether their values are the same as mine, it may have gone differently.

As I mentioned earlier, surrounding yourself with people who are likeminded is important to your success, as well. From this experience, I learned that you have to do your homework. You have to have your building blocks.

If I could go back, I would've gone and sat in other restaurants and talked to other restaurant managers. I would have really interviewed co-partners a little more diligently and screened them more carefully to make sure that it was really going to be a good fit before losing my time, my money – and my mind.

If something like this has happened to you, it is important to refuse to succumb to the idea that you are a failure. Failure only means that there is something that you need to improve. It doesn't mean you quit. Failure is there to help us learn from our experiences.

Even though that dream didn't work out for me, it doesn't mean that I lost interest or a desire to possibly ever have a restaurant again. However, if I ever did go into it again, I would do many things differently.

Plans don't always go according to schedule, but they can still be an essential part to making/building your dreams into reality. Even though I am a dreamer, I am also more of a realist. I dream all day long, but if I can't see it on paper, if I can't map it out and turn it into a goal that has achievable steps and outcomes, then it's not for me.

Being a dreamer is needed, but you also need to be what I call a "Dream Transformist." Dreamers just stay with the dream, and they stop there, but a dream transformist uses the dream and then puts it into a realistic place.

Last week, I sat down with two very different employees to discuss performance issues and things that are lacking in their current job status.

I met a young woman who was in our billing department at the facility. She told me, "When I'm doing billing and collections, my favorite part of it is having a conversation with the patient. I love talking to the patient, and then they tell me what's going on in their world, what even brought them to this emergency room that day. We end up building a relationship together, and I figure out how I can help them with their bill."

In having a dream transformist mindset, I told her, "You know what? This is a phenomenal role that we don't currently have in our organization."

She was describing a patient advocate role. The position would be to create an experience for the patient, and then talk to them about that experience, and then talk to them about what's going on. If they have an issue with something that's going on outside of what brought them into our healthcare system, we'd find out how we can help them with it.

This employee would advocate for them, and be in charge of their patient experience, amenity-wise, facility-wise, billing-wise, that impacts health care.

I created a role for this one person, and that was her passion – her dream – that we were able to transform into a reality. It was a win-win.

Taking care of patients is just the simple part of what we do. I can go in, and I can take care of a patient medically. That's easy. That's expected. However, it's all this other stuff that we do for our patients that create an experience for them.

The dreams within you are meant to be realized, you just need to plan out how to attain them.

TO THINK ABOUT

1. What might be one hazard of postponing a trial run of someone's dream?

2. Consider three jobs that you enjoyed (even volunteer positions would work). Are there some common threads, or aspects of the jobs that you enjoyed, that could point you to a specific position that would be exciting to you?

3. As you think about a dream that is developing in your mind, imagine one outcome that would be positive, and one that would be negative.

4. Think of three positives that might actually emerge from that negative. These can be positive outcomes for yourself and for your loved ones.

CHAPTER 5:
Exploration

"Who looks outside dreams; who looks inside awakes."
... But your vision will become clear only when you can look into your own heart."
Carl Jung

Part of exploring, dipping your toes out there, feeling what is possible may look like taking a personality test, reading, journaling, or soul searching for something that makes you feel the most fulfilled.

You may already have the dream, but it's important to explore by having the mindset that this isn't the end-all, be-all.

It's okay to test the waters before you jump right in. You need to find out what you like, what you don't like, and then determine what it is that feeds your soul.

Writing with the intention to tell your story in your own words has proven to be helpful in determining your life's purpose. According to a 2008 study, when we feel meaning and purpose in our lives, it helps us define a clear narrative to share with others of what we've learned and how we've grown. As we overcome obstacles and can share of these stories of victory with others, we can make a deeper impact because we better understand how using our strengths can change the world, one story at a time.[3]

When thinking about yourself in a narrative, how do you think an author would describe you? What is it that makes you, you?

Self-exploration in this way is one of the best ways to determine where you see yourself in this world. What is it that makes your soul feel fed?

Many employees in my line of work haven't explored exactly what it is that can make them happy to go to work every day. In many instances, I make an effort to sit down with some of my colleagues and do an assessment surrounded by what they love about the job as well as what they don't love in order to learn more about their inner yearnings for their careers.

In some cases, personal assessments such as the Myers-Briggs personality test offers a substantial insight into who they are as a person and what makes them the most fulfilled in a career.

For instance, you may have felt an inclination to become a teacher, but results from your personality test may show that you most likely wouldn't be happy taking care of small children.

If you have never explored your personality before, it is something that can be very enlightening and aid you on your journey of exploration.

Scientifically speaking, your personality can make it incredibly seamless to work in one occupation, yet incredibly difficult to work in others. In order to be content and fulfilled in your occupation, it is vital to match your purpose and work environment with your personality type.

The Myers-Briggs personality test is a self-reporting questionnaire that indicates different psychological preferences of the human mind; it determines how people perceive the world and make decisions. The test is based on the conceptual theory proposed by the famous Swiss psychiatrist Carl Jung who speculated that people view the world differently.

Specifically, they view the world using the four principal psychological functions of sensation, intuition, feeling, and thinking. The mother-daughter duo of Katharine Cook Briggs and Isabel Briggs Myers, who developed the test, determined that one of these functions will be dominant in every person, and that function determines the way that individual moves through their career as well as life, in general.

In taking the free test, one will be able to see their four principal functions that determine whether they are more extroverted or introverted, more sensing or more oriented toward intuition, whether they think more or feel more, as well as whether they judge more or perceive more in their day to day lives.

If you are stuck in a cycle of thinking that you are a failure who is not living their life to the fullest, it may simply be due to the fact that you are not yet in alignment with who you really are.

For example, according to various studies of the different types, ENTPs are great visionaries and leaders, INTJs often find themselves in engineering roles, and ISFPs often work in people-oriented industries. In each case, the individual's characteristics make the occupation a good match.

All this to say, the free Myers-Briggs test online can be helpful in determining what it is that makes you, you.

Another assessment that I love is "The Color Code" created by Dr. Taylor Hartman which divides personalities into four colors while informing you of your most dominant color: red (motivated by power), yellow (motivated by fun), blue (motivated by intimacy), or white (motivated by peace).

In taking the assessment, the questions are framed to be answered by how you would best describe yourself as a child. In the full profile assessment available, the assessment takes your personality and tells you how you work with other personalities. In this way, you are better aligned to understand varying personality types in the professional world.

The Color Code can be enlightening in uncovering how to resolve conflicts if you are a yellow, and you suspect someone else is a blue. Just as well, if you are a blue and they are a red, how do you work together on a team project efficiently?

The Color Code really gives you some ideas of how different personalities can work together in different situations and be very successful.

Other personality tests include the DiSC assessment, which helps you see where you land within four quadrants: dominance, influence, steadiness and compliance. It is popular as a career assessment and many companies ask their employees to take it.

As much as a dreamer thinks that they can go out and achieve their dream all on their own, at some point we all must, at some point, interact, intertwine, and depend on others in order to be successful.

This is especially important with regard to children. The reality is that someday you will not be there for your children anymore, and they need to know that they have a system around them that can meet their needs outside of their mother and father.

In serving yourself by going after your dreams, you're also giving your family the opportunity to be served in a bigger way.

When you follow your dreams as well as understand those around you in a more in-depth way, your family will start to understand that the sun doesn't rise and fall with you. (This can be painful to consider, especially for young mothers who enjoy being needed. Nobody would argue that raising children is not easy.)

But to be sure, nobody is asking you to change the comfortable workings of their family. You are not leaving them! It's *because* your family is the most important thing in the world to you that you are wanting to know what else is out there in the world for yourself, for them, so you can show them, teach them, and guide them in the right direction.

By exploring your dream, you become a role model to your children. Everyone says to their children "go after your dreams" and "you can be anything you set your mind to," but they're only going to truly believe those statements if your actions have backed up that assertion. Your children must know that those words aren't only words.

Without a doubt, exploring your dreams will only make you a better mother for your children. Every experience that you have is an experience that you can bring back to your children to give them guidance and wisdom.

Thoughts

TO THINK ABOUT

1. Investigate the following online personality assessments.

2. Complete two of them.

3. Review your results. Do they seem accurate?

4. Can you use the results toward honing in on your dream?

- ☑ Myers-Briggs: https://www.truity.com/test/type-finder-personality-test-new
- ☑ Enneagram https://www.truity.com/test/enneagram-personality-test
- ☑ DiSC: https://www.truity.com/test/disc-personality-test

CHAPTER 6:

The Benefits of Failure

> "It is impossible to live without failing at something, unless you live so cautiously that you might as well not have lived at all – in which case, you fail by default."
>
> J.K. Rowling

The other night, I went to my daughter's volleyball practice. My daughter has real struggles with self-esteem and being confident in what she does. I suddenly realized that every time she made a mistake on the volleyball court, she turned to her coach and said, "Oh, I'm sorry. Oh, I'm sorry. I'm sorry."

Her coach finally said, "You know what? I want you to have a conversation with your mom. Your mom is a CEO of a company, and I want you to have a conversation with your mom about what happens when employees, or people that she works with, make a mistake."

My daughter walked up to me and said, "Okay, Mom, what happens when people make a mistake?"

I told her, "Well, first of all, for them to say I'm sorry to me, really – that doesn't help us any. If there was a mistake that was made, if there was something that was missed, something we didn't do, telling me that they're sorry really doesn't help the situation."

I explained to her that what I need them to do is recognize what went wrong, and fix it. I find much more confidence in that person to be able to do their job.

So, as you go forward and you get a job, you need to fix your mistakes rather than apologize for them.

Simply apologizing for making mistakes doesn't move anything forward in the workplace. If you hurt someone's feelings, then you say that you're sorry, but if it's something that you have accountability and responsibility over, then there's no need to say that you're sorry because it's not recognizing what you did wrong and it doesn't fix the problem.

If you don't recognize what you did wrong on the volleyball serve when you missed it, and fix it on the next one, then you don't ever get any better, you don't learn from your mistake, and you don't move forward.

Apologizing in and of itself shows a lack of confidence in yourself and your ability to be able to move forward.

Without the life lessons that I've had in my experience, I may not have been able to share those exact words with my daughter about confidence.

The next morning, my daughter asked me, "Are you confident at work Mom?" and I told her, "Most days I'm very confident about what I do and the decisions that I make. However, I may make the wrong decisions, but I'm always confident about the fact that I'm going to make wrong decisions."

The difference, I explained, is that I know that I can learn from those wrong decisions. I know that I can move forward.

Every time you take responsibility for your mistakes and fix them, your confidence will grow. It's unrealistic to think that you would ever get confidence unless you experiment, test, put yourself out there, and allow yourself to make mistakes. This is how you learn, how you grow, and how you build confidence.

There are so many benefits of failure. You cannot go into all of your choices with an intense fear of failure, because then you've already set yourself up to fail. You have to go into it knowing that you're going to try your hardest, and if you don't succeed, well then what does that mean to you?

How are you going to move forward? That's the only thing that matters. Be confident in your ability to deal with failure before it even happens.

So many of us get caught up in our ideas of perfectionism. As much as I try to say that I'm not a perfectionist, I know that I probably am – although, to me, perfectionism is knowing that I did a task to my satisfaction.

If it is that I went into something knowing that I may not succeed – and I am okay with it taking a different path, and it does end up taking a different path – then it was, in my eyes, the way that I could deal with it: it was perfection, per se.

Perfection, to me, is really more of just a really high level of expectations. It's not that you never make mistakes, but if you do make them, you fix them, and then, as long as you're recognizing mistakes and fixing them, then that is just as good as being perfect, to me.

Perfectionism is your ability to give it your all. For better or for worse, if you gave it your all, then you were striving for that perfection.

If you're using perfectionism as an excuse to procrastinate or deny your dreams, then you're never going to get the magic of what this chapter is all about, which is: when you go out there, when you start to experiment, you will see what you like and what you don't like. You will learn so much about yourself and those around you, then you are able to find that inner drive and motivation to keep you going for it.

When I'm starting a new project, or when I have a new idea, I put all of my goals down on paper, strictly in pencil. I always do it in pencil because it is inevitable that your goals and ideas will change.

It may change hours from now or months from now, but you have to be able to erase that solid line and make a dotted line.

Drawing up your plans in pencil gives you the ability to erase them, because they will change.

If it's in pencil, it's shapeable, and it's changeable. You know that it's not permanent; you can change it as you go along, as you learn more, as you discover, as you explore.

It all starts with a blank sheet of paper. I take everything that's in my mind, and I start writing everything down. A lot of times, they're in boxes, or they're in shapes, as a part of that big idea.

If it's a person, it's a certain kind of shape. If it's a process, it may be a line. If it's moving from the left side of the page to the right side of the page or the top to the bottom, it's however I get

Thoughts
TO THINK ABOUT

1. Would you consider yourself a high achiever who enjoys accomplishment?

2. Why is self-care an area of oversight that can be difficult for this type of individual?

3. What are your most effective ways to de-stress and unwind?

4. Share your thoughts about the accuracy and importance of the statement mentioned in this chapter:

    "...it's not about how hard you push yourself, it's about how well you recover and recharge from life's blows."

What will happen after you raise your children? Now what? Who will you be once your children are raised and out on their own?

It is so important to raise your children and be that stability for them, but you are more than just a parent. You're you. You're a writer. You're a teacher. You're an author, an entrepreneur, a doctor, a nurse - whatever you want to be. You must get the most out of life while you are here. When you live out your dreams, your mind broadens and you learn more about yourself, about life.

As I said before, making the decision to go after my dreams has made me a better mom to my children. The joy I get from achieving my dream has made me walk a little taller, proud of what I bring to the table each day to teach my children.

Making the choice to go out into the world, to have experiences working in an organization, starting a business, healing others as a nurse, and caring for people is the best choice that I ever made for myself and my children.

There is nothing like caring for a sick and dying person in the most vulnerable moment of their life and doing my best to take those experiences back home to use as a reference in teaching my children about life.

It's not what you say to your children, it's who you are when you're with your children and who you are when you're not with them.

As Gandhi famously said, "Your life is your message, not the words that come out of your mouth." You influence your children and teach them by showing them how you choose to live your life. If you go after your dreams, they will see the example that you have set.

The other day my son said, "Mom, wow, I wish I could do that like you. You're just so good at things like that."

I turned to him and I said, "Son, I wasn't always good at things like this. I had to go out and figure out how to do these things over time, and I learned. It's not that I'm just naturally good at it. I learned by life experiences how to *become* good at it."

Similarly, my daughter was at a speech competition and told me, "Mom, I just need to have confidence like you. You always stand up and talk to people with no problem."

I could not believe that my children viewed me this way, when I didn't feel this way about myself in the past. It's not like I was born with confidence. It's practice. It's from having to stand up and speak to big groups of people so often.

I always try to reinforce the idea in my daughter that, if she can stand up in front of middle school and high school students, she can stand up in front of anybody in the world.

As long as you stand up with your shoulders back and your head held high, you can say what you need to say confidently. Life is not about being great from the get-go, it's about your ability to keep going and practicing when you aren't great yet.

If you are still in that cycle of saying, "I wish I could do this, but it's not in the cards for me," I'm speaking to you, giving you a little shake and saying, "Sure you can." You can start with small things.

Ask me any questions that you may have. I would love to share with you how I felt just like you once before. Maybe how I got there isn't exactly how you will get there, but maybe it will give you some guidance or a different way to think about how you could do it. In this final chapter, I invite you to continue this journey that you have started.

I want you to say yes to your dreams and yes to being a mom. No need to sacrifice anything in your life - you *can* have both. If all of us as women unlearn all that we have learned from past society and our oppressed history, we would see the confidence of women and the confidence of young women come to life like we haven't yet seen ever before.

We will see more women CEOs, more women in the House and Senate, more women making the world better than the way we found it. We must not forget that our world is still male-dominated and male-controlled.

We must show our young girls our confidence. We must show them that there are great role models out there for anything that they want to be. I don't want to ever hear my daughter say the words, "I can't do that because I'm a girl - no one would take me seriously or respect me if I tried to do that."

As a collective generation, let us not let the same voices that discouraged us growing up discourage our young girls in the same way.

Let us be the moms that end the trajectory set out for them. Our society will rapidly change when we as women encourage other women and encourage each other's children to shine, dream big, and go for it.

If we have learned anything from Rosie the Riveter, it's that we are here to tell one another that "we can do it." We can get to the top of that corporate ladder by taking turns lifting each other up.

If you see a mom working late nights, exhausted by doing it all, offer to drop their kids off at school for some of the week. Fight for her dreams and she will fight for yours, too. We are all sisters here and sisters help each other get ahead.

When we go about life from our hearts and help women get ahead together, it builds a network for our children and it shows the teamwork of humanity.

Maybe my kids have a question that they don't feel comfortable asking me, but that mom that I team-share with, maybe they will feel comfortable to ask her. I want my kids to have resources when they have problems.

I don't want them to feel isolated, feeling like they only have mom and dad to ask, and when it comes to something that they don't feel comfortable, they have nobody to go to.

We are all here on this earth together for a reason. We are meant to help one another. Let's collectively accept that help.

I truly believe that God has given everybody a servant's heart to care for one another. You can care for your neighbor with the unique opportunity and talent that only you have.

You have been given a heart to serve others. To help your family, yes, that is part of it, but in the grander scheme of things, to use it to help a stranger, to empathize and love one another unconditionally.

Go after your dreams fervently and love each other with all you've got, then nothing will be wasted!

TO THINK ABOUT

1. In what specific, small or big ways can making your dream become a reality affect your daughters?

2. In what specific, small or big ways can making your dream become a reality affect your sons?

3. How can the success of your family and your Business of Mom be leveraged to give other mothers success with their own families and their own businesses? Be specific.

4. How do you feel that your help given to the other mothers would benefit you?

Endnotes

1 – Chapter 3, page 30

According to a Harvard Business School study:

Dina Gerdeman, "Kids of Working Moms Grow into Happy Adults," July 16, 2018, https://hbswk.hbs.edu/item/kids-of-working-moms-grow-into-happy-adults

2- Chapter 4, page 38

Research has found that vivid, written descriptions:

Murphy, Mark. "Neuroscience Explains Why You Need To Write Down Your Goals If You Actually Want To Achieve Them." Forbes. Forbes Magazine, April 15, 2018. https://www.forbes.com/sites/markmurphy/2018/04/15/neuroscience-explains-why-you-need-to-write-down-your-goals-if-you-actually-want-to-achieve-them/

3- Chapter 5, pages 45-46

Writing with the intention to tell your story:

S.. Ackerman, D.. Zuroff, M.J.. Ross G.W.. Allport, G.A.. Bonanno J.J.. Bauer, D.P.. McAdams J.J.. Bauer, D.P.. McAdams J.J.. Bauer, J.A.. Singer P.S.. Blagov, J.. Gluck S.. Bluck, et al. "Narrative Identity and Eudaimonic Well-Being." Journal of Happiness Studies. Springer Netherlands, January 1, 1970. https://link.springer.com/article/10.1007/s10902-006-9021-6

4 – Chapter 12, pages 114-115

A New York Times article detailed:

Bennett, Jessica. "What Makes a Leader?" The New York Times. The New York Times, June 17, 2019. https://www.nytimes.com/2019/06/17/business/women-power-leadership.html.

Made in the USA
Columbia, SC
10 February 2021